Chapter 1: Introduction to AI in Marketing

The Evolution of Marketing

The evolution of marketing has undergone significant transformations over the decades, shaped by technological advancements, changing consumer behaviors, and emerging trends. In the early days, marketing primarily relied on direct sales techniques and face-to-face interactions. Businesses utilized print media, such as newspapers and brochures, to reach potential customers. This traditional approach focused on product features and benefits, often neglecting the nuances of consumer preferences. As the marketplace became more competitive, the need for a more strategic approach to marketing became evident.

The introduction of radio and television in the mid-20th century revolutionized marketing strategies. Advertisers began to recognize the power of storytelling and visual engagement, which allowed brands to connect emotionally with their audiences. This era saw the rise of mass marketing, where companies aimed to reach as many consumers as possible through captivating advertisements. However, this one-size-fits-all approach often led to inefficiencies, as businesses struggled to target specific demographics effectively.

With the advent of the internet in the late 20th century, the marketing landscape transformed once again. Digital marketing emerged as a powerful tool, enabling businesses to engage with consumers in real-time. Search engines, social media platforms, and email marketing became essential components of marketing strategies. This shift allowed for more personalized communication, as businesses could segment their audiences and tailor their messages accordingly. The ability to track consumer behavior online further enhanced marketers' understanding of their target markets.

The rise of data analytics marked a pivotal moment in the evolution of marketing. Businesses began to leverage data to inform their strategies, leading to more informed decision-making and improved campaign performance. The integration of customer insights into marketing efforts enabled companies to predict trends, optimize their messaging, and enhance customer experiences. However, the sheer volume of data generated also presented challenges, as marketers needed to navigate through complex information to extract actionable insights.

Today, the emergence of artificial intelligence is driving the next phase in the evolution of marketing. AI technologies are enabling businesses to automate processes, analyze vast amounts of data, and provide personalized experiences at scale. Machine learning algorithms are being used to predict consumer behavior, optimize ad placements, and enhance customer service through chatbots and virtual assistants. As AI continues to evolve, it offers unprecedented opportunities for businesses to gain a competitive advantage by fostering deeper connections with consumers and driving innovation in marketing strategies.

Understanding AI and Its Capabilities

Artificial Intelligence (AI) has rapidly transformed various sectors, and its impact on marketing and advertising is particularly profound. At its core, AI refers to the simulation of human intelligence processes by machines, particularly computer systems. This includes the ability to learn from data, reason, and self-correct. In marketing, AI technologies can analyze vast amounts of data to identify patterns, predict consumer behavior, and personalize experiences, ultimately leading to more effective strategies and campaigns.

Understanding the capabilities of AI begins with recognizing its various applications in marketing and advertising. One of the most significant advantages of AI is its ability to process and analyze data at an unprecedented scale. Traditional data analysis methods often struggle with the volume and complexity of modern consumer data.

AI, on the other hand, can sift through large datasets in real-time, providing marketers with insights that were previously unattainable. This capability allows businesses to make data-driven decisions, optimizing their marketing strategies based on consumer preferences and behaviors.

Another essential aspect of AI in marketing is its role in automation. AI-powered tools can automate repetitive tasks such as email marketing, social media posting, and customer segmentation. This automation not only enhances efficiency but also frees up valuable time for marketing professionals to focus on more strategic initiatives. Additionally, chatbots and virtual assistants, powered by natural language processing, can engage with customers in real-time, providing immediate responses to inquiries and enhancing the overall customer experience.

Personalization is another critical benefit of AI in marketing. Consumers today expect personalized experiences tailored to their individual preferences. AI enables businesses to deliver targeted content, product recommendations, and promotional offers based on data-driven insights. Machine learning algorithms can analyze consumer behavior and adjust marketing messages accordingly, ensuring that each interaction is relevant and engaging. This level of personalization fosters stronger customer relationships and drives higher conversion rates.

Finally, the predictive capabilities of AI are revolutionizing how businesses approach marketing strategies. By analyzing historical data and identifying trends, AI can forecast future consumer behaviors and market shifts. Marketers can leverage these insights to anticipate customer needs and adjust their campaigns proactively. This predictive analytics approach allows businesses to stay ahead of the competition, ensuring that they are not only responsive to current trends but also prepared for future developments in the marketplace. As AI continues to evolve, its integration into marketing and advertising will undoubtedly offer even greater opportunities for innovation and competitive advantage.

The Need for a Marketing Revolution

The landscape of marketing is undergoing a profound transformation driven by the rapid advancement of artificial intelligence. Traditional marketing strategies, which often relied on broad demographic targeting and generalized messaging, are proving inadequate in an era where consumers expect personalized experiences. This shift highlights the urgent need for a marketing revolution that harnesses the capabilities of AI to create more targeted, efficient, and impactful marketing campaigns. As businesses navigate this changing environment, understanding the role of AI in reshaping marketing practices becomes essential for maintaining a competitive edge.

One of the most significant advantages of AI in marketing is its ability to analyze vast amounts of data quickly and accurately. Businesses can leverage AI algorithms to parse through consumer behavior data, social media interactions, and purchasing patterns in real-time. This analysis enables companies to identify trends and preferences that would be impossible to discern manually. By utilizing AI-driven insights, marketers can segment their audiences more precisely, leading to tailored campaigns that resonate on a personal level with potential customers. In this way, AI not only enhances targeting but also improves overall customer satisfaction by delivering relevant content.

Furthermore, AI technologies empower marketers to automate various processes, freeing up valuable time and resources. Tasks such as customer segmentation, content creation, and campaign optimization can now be performed by AI systems, allowing marketing teams to focus on strategy and creative development. Automation also enhances efficiency, reducing the likelihood of human error and enabling campaigns to be executed at a scale that was previously unattainable. This newfound efficiency means that businesses can respond more swiftly to market changes, staying ahead of competitors who may still rely on traditional, slower methods of marketing execution.

The integration of AI also fosters a deeper understanding of the customer journey. By employing machine learning algorithms, businesses can track and analyze customer interactions across multiple touchpoints, from initial awareness through to post-purchase behavior. This comprehensive view allows marketers to identify pain points and opportunities for improvement throughout the customer experience. As a result, brands can optimize their marketing strategies to better align with customer needs and preferences, ultimately leading to increased loyalty and higher conversion rates.

Finally, the need for a marketing revolution is underscored by the growing importance of data privacy and ethical considerations in marketing practices. As consumers become more aware of how their data is used, businesses must navigate a landscape that prioritizes transparency and trust. AI can play a crucial role in ensuring compliance with regulations and in fostering ethical marketing practices. By utilizing AI to manage data responsibly and engage consumers in meaningful ways, businesses can build stronger relationships with their audiences. This approach not only addresses consumer concerns but also positions companies as leaders in ethical marketing, further enhancing their competitive advantage in the marketplace.

Chapter 2: The Role of AI in Consumer Insights

Data Collection and Analysis

Data collection and analysis are fundamental components of leveraging artificial intelligence in marketing and advertising. In today's data-driven landscape, businesses must gather and interpret vast amounts of information to enhance their marketing strategies effectively. The first step in this process involves identifying the specific data sources that are relevant to the business's marketing objectives. These sources can range from customer demographics and purchasing behavior to social media interactions and website analytics. By systematically collecting data from these various sources, businesses can create a comprehensive picture of their target audience, which is crucial for informed decision-making.

Once the data is collected, the next phase is analysis. This involves employing advanced analytical tools and techniques to derive insights from the raw data. AI technologies, such as machine learning algorithms, can process large datasets more efficiently than traditional methods. These algorithms can identify patterns and trends that may not be immediately apparent, allowing marketers to make predictions about consumer behavior. For instance, predictive analytics can help businesses anticipate which products will be in demand, enabling them to optimize inventory and marketing efforts.

Furthermore, sentiment analysis is another vital aspect of data analysis in marketing. By evaluating customer feedback, reviews, and social media mentions, businesses can gauge public perception of their brand. AI-driven sentiment analysis tools can categorize sentiments as positive, negative, or neutral, providing valuable insights into customer satisfaction and brand reputation. This information can inform marketing campaigns, helping businesses to tailor their messaging and improve customer engagement.

Data visualization tools play a critical role in translating complex analytical results into actionable insights. By presenting data in an easily digestible format, such as graphs or dashboards, business professionals can quickly grasp key performance indicators and trends. This visualization aids in communicating findings to stakeholders effectively, ensuring that everyone involved understands the implications of the data. Enhanced visualization capabilities also facilitate real-time monitoring of marketing campaigns, allowing businesses to pivot strategies based on immediate feedback.

Lastly, ethical considerations in data collection and analysis cannot be overlooked. As businesses leverage AI to gather and analyze data, they must navigate privacy concerns and ensure compliance with regulations such as GDPR. Transparency in data practices builds trust with consumers and can enhance brand loyalty. By prioritizing ethical data practices, businesses not only comply with legal standards but also position themselves as responsible entities in the marketplace. This commitment to ethics, combined with effective data collection and analysis, ultimately drives sustainable competitive advantage in the rapidly evolving marketing landscape.

Predictive Analytics and Customer Behavior

Predictive analytics has emerged as a transformative technology in the realm of marketing and advertising, enabling businesses to anticipate customer needs and behaviors with unprecedented accuracy. By leveraging vast amounts of historical data and advanced algorithms, companies can identify patterns that inform future customer actions. This capability allows businesses to tailor their marketing strategies, ensuring they reach the right audience with the right message at the right time. As competition intensifies, organizations that effectively harness predictive analytics can gain a significant edge over their rivals.

Understanding customer behavior is central to developing effective marketing strategies. Predictive analytics provides insights into consumer preferences, purchasing patterns, and engagement levels. By analyzing data from various sources, such as social media, e-commerce transactions, and customer feedback, marketers can create detailed customer profiles. These profiles not only reveal who the customers are but also predict how they are likely to engage with products or services in the future. This deep understanding of customer behavior allows businesses to craft personalized marketing campaigns that resonate more deeply with their target audience.

Moreover, predictive analytics can significantly enhance customer segmentation efforts. Traditional segmentation methods often rely on broad demographic categories, which may not accurately reflect the nuances of consumer behavior. Predictive models, on the other hand, can segment customers based on their likelihood to respond to specific marketing initiatives, their propensity to churn, or their potential lifetime value. This granular approach allows marketers to allocate resources more efficiently, targeting high-potential segments with tailored offers that are more likely to convert.

The implementation of predictive analytics also facilitates real-time decision-making in marketing campaigns. As data is continuously collected and analyzed, businesses can adjust their strategies on the fly, responding to changes in customer behavior or market conditions. For example, if predictive models indicate a sudden increase in demand for a specific product, marketers can quickly ramp up promotional efforts, ensuring they capitalize on the trend before it dissipates. This agility not only enhances campaign effectiveness but also improves overall customer satisfaction, as businesses can respond to consumer needs promptly.

In conclusion, the integration of predictive analytics into marketing and advertising strategies represents a paradigm shift for business professionals. By utilizing data-driven insights to understand and anticipate customer behavior, organizations can create more effective marketing campaigns that are not only personalized but also adaptive to real-time market dynamics. As businesses continue to embrace AI and predictive analytics, those who invest in these technologies will likely emerge as leaders in their respective industries, setting new standards for customer engagement and satisfaction.

Personalization Through AI

Personalization through AI has emerged as a transformative force in the marketing and advertising landscape. Businesses are increasingly recognizing that customer expectations have shifted toward a demand for tailored experiences. AI technologies enable organizations to analyze vast amounts of data, identify patterns, and generate insights that facilitate hyper-personalized marketing strategies. By leveraging AI, businesses can create targeted campaigns that resonate with individual consumers, enhancing engagement and driving conversions.

One of the most significant advantages of AI in personalization is its ability to process and interpret customer data at an unprecedented scale. Machine learning algorithms can analyze behavioral data, purchase history, and demographic information to segment audiences more effectively. This allows marketers to design personalized content and offers that align with the unique preferences of different consumer segments. As a result, organizations can move away from a one-size-fits-all approach and cultivate deeper connections with their customers.

Moreover, predictive analytics powered by AI plays a crucial role in shaping personalized marketing efforts. By forecasting customer behavior and preferences, businesses can proactively tailor their messaging and product recommendations. For instance, recommendation engines utilized by e-commerce platforms analyze user interactions to suggest products that align with individual tastes. This not only enhances the shopping experience for customers but also increases the likelihood of upselling and cross-selling opportunities for businesses.

AI-driven personalization extends beyond product recommendations to encompass various marketing channels, including email, social media, and web content. Marketers can use AI to automate the creation of personalized email campaigns that cater to the interests of individual recipients. Social media platforms also benefit from AI algorithms that curate content based on user engagement patterns, allowing brands to deliver relevant advertisements to specific demographics. This level of customization fosters a sense of connection and loyalty between consumers and brands, ultimately driving repeat business.

In conclusion, the integration of AI into marketing strategies is redefining the concept of personalization. By harnessing the power of AI, businesses can create customized experiences that not only meet but exceed customer expectations. As technology continues to evolve, the potential for AI to enhance personalization in marketing and advertising will only grow. For business professionals, embracing these advancements is essential to staying competitive in an increasingly dynamic marketplace where consumer preferences are constantly changing.

Chapter 3: AI-Powered Content Creation

Automated Content Generation

Automated content generation has emerged as a transformative force in the marketing landscape, enabling businesses to produce high volumes of content efficiently and effectively. With advancements in artificial intelligence, organizations can now automate the creation of various content types, from blog posts and social media updates to email newsletters and product descriptions. This technology not only accelerates the content creation process but also ensures that the output is tailored to specific audience segments, enhancing relevance and engagement.

One of the primary advantages of automated content generation is its ability to analyze vast amounts of data to inform content strategies. AI systems can evaluate consumer behavior, preferences, and trends, allowing marketers to generate content that resonates with their target audiences. By leveraging data-driven insights, businesses can create personalized experiences that increase customer engagement and drive conversions. This capability is particularly valuable in today's fast-paced digital environment, where timely and relevant content is essential for maintaining competitive advantage.

Furthermore, automated content generation tools often incorporate natural language processing and machine learning algorithms, which enable them to produce human-like text. These tools can adapt to different tones, styles, and formats, ensuring that the generated content aligns with brand voice and messaging. As a result, businesses can maintain consistency across their marketing channels while scaling their content production efforts. This level of automation not only saves time and resources but also allows marketing teams to focus on strategic initiatives rather than routine content tasks.

Despite the many benefits, there are challenges associated with automated content generation that businesses must navigate. One significant concern is the potential for quality control issues. While AI has made significant strides in content generation, it is not infallible. Businesses need to implement robust review processes to ensure that the generated content meets their quality standards and aligns with their brand values. Moreover, marketers should remain vigilant about the ethical implications of using AI in content creation, particularly concerning originality and potential biases present in the training data.

In conclusion, automated content generation presents a powerful opportunity for businesses to enhance their marketing efforts and improve operational efficiency. By harnessing the capabilities of AI, organizations can produce personalized, relevant, and timely content that engages their audience effectively. However, to fully leverage this technology, businesses must address the associated challenges and maintain a balance between automation and human oversight. As the marketing landscape continues to evolve, those who embrace automated content generation will be well-positioned to gain a competitive edge in the marketplace.

AI in Copywriting and Ad Design

The integration of artificial intelligence in copywriting and ad design has revolutionized the marketing landscape, providing businesses with innovative tools to enhance their creative processes and optimize advertising strategies. AI technologies, such as natural language processing and machine learning, enable marketers to generate high-quality content at scale, reducing the time and effort traditionally required in these areas. By analyzing vast amounts of data, AI can identify trends, consumer preferences, and effective messaging, allowing brands to craft compelling narratives that resonate with their target audiences.

One of the key benefits of AI in copywriting is its ability to produce tailored content based on user behavior and demographics. AI-driven platforms can analyze customer interactions across various touchpoints, enabling marketers to create personalized messages that engage consumers on a deeper level. This level of customization not only increases the effectiveness of marketing campaigns but also enhances customer satisfaction and loyalty. As a result, businesses can achieve higher conversion rates and maximize their return on investment.

In ad design, AI tools can streamline the creative process by automating repetitive tasks and providing data-driven insights. Machine learning algorithms can assess the performance of different ad formats and visuals, suggesting modifications that improve engagement and click-through rates. Moreover, AI can facilitate A/B testing by rapidly generating and analyzing multiple design variations, enabling marketers to identify the most effective approaches without the lengthy trial-and-error process typical in traditional advertising.

Moreover, AI can enhance collaboration between creative teams and data analysts. By merging creative intuition with data insights, businesses can develop campaigns that not only look good but are also strategically sound. AI tools can offer predictive analytics that forecast the potential success of a campaign based on historical data and market trends, allowing teams to make informed decisions about their strategies. This collaboration fosters a more agile marketing environment where adjustments can be made in real-time, ensuring that campaigns remain relevant and impactful.

As AI continues to evolve, its role in copywriting and ad design will likely expand further, opening new avenues for innovation in marketing. Business professionals must stay abreast of these advancements to leverage AI effectively and maintain a competitive advantage in their respective industries. Embracing AI not only enhances operational efficiency but also empowers teams to explore creative possibilities that were previously unattainable, ultimately transforming the way brands communicate and connect with their audiences.

Enhancing Creativity with AI Tools

Artificial Intelligence (AI) tools have emerged as powerful allies in enhancing creativity within the marketing and advertising sectors. Business professionals are increasingly recognizing that these technologies not only streamline processes but also unlock new avenues for innovative thinking. By integrating AI tools into their creative workflows, marketers can harness data-driven insights and generate fresh ideas that resonate with target audiences. This transformation is crucial in a landscape where consumer preferences are continually evolving, and brands must differentiate themselves to remain competitive.

One of the primary ways AI enhances creativity is through data analysis and trend identification. AI algorithms can sift through vast amounts of data, identifying patterns that human marketers may overlook. By analyzing consumer behavior, social media trends, and market dynamics, AI tools can provide actionable insights that inform creative strategies. This data-driven approach allows marketers to craft campaigns that are not only innovative but also grounded in real-time consumer preferences, leading to more effective messaging and engagement.

Moreover, AI tools can assist in the brainstorming process, generating ideas and concepts that can serve as a foundation for creative projects. Advanced AI systems use natural language processing and machine learning to understand existing content, allowing them to propose new themes, slogans, or visual concepts. This capability can be particularly beneficial during the early stages of campaign development, where the pressure for originality is high. By leveraging AI for idea generation, marketing professionals can explore a broader range of possibilities and push the boundaries of conventional creativity.

AI also plays a critical role in personalizing marketing efforts, which inherently enhances creativity. With AI's ability to analyze individual consumer data, marketers can create tailored experiences that resonate on a personal level. This personalization extends beyond simple demographic targeting; it includes understanding a consumer's interests, preferences, and behaviors. By utilizing AI tools to deliver customized content, brands can forge deeper connections with their audience, ultimately leading to more impactful and creative advertising efforts that stand out in a crowded marketplace.

Finally, the collaboration between human creativity and AI capabilities fosters an environment of innovation. Rather than replacing the creative process, AI enhances it by providing tools that allow marketers to experiment and iterate quickly. This synergy can lead to more daring and effective campaigns, as professionals are empowered to explore unconventional ideas without the fear of failure. As AI continues to evolve, its role in the marketing and advertising landscape will likely expand, enabling business professionals to leverage these advancements for sustained competitive advantage.

Chapter 4: AI in Social Media Marketing

Social Listening and Sentiment Analysis

Social listening and sentiment analysis have emerged as pivotal components in the landscape of modern marketing, particularly as businesses strive to enhance their understanding of consumer behavior and preferences. Social listening involves monitoring social media platforms and online conversations to gain insights into what customers are saying about a brand, product, or service. This practice allows companies to track mentions, identify trends, and engage with their audience in real-time. By tapping into the wealth of data generated on social media, businesses can refine their marketing strategies, develop better products, and foster stronger relationships with their customers.

Sentiment analysis, often integrated with social listening efforts, provides a deeper layer of understanding by evaluating the emotional tone behind online conversations. This process utilizes natural language processing (NLP) and machine learning algorithms to analyze text data and categorize sentiments as positive, negative, or neutral. By leveraging sentiment analysis, brands can gauge public perception and identify potential issues before they escalate. This proactive approach enables marketing teams to address customer concerns, manage brand reputation, and enhance overall customer satisfaction.

The integration of AI technologies into social listening and sentiment analysis significantly amplifies their effectiveness. Traditional methods of data collection and analysis can be time-consuming and prone to human error. However, AI-driven tools can process vast amounts of data quickly and accurately, uncovering insights that would be difficult to discern otherwise. These tools can identify patterns and trends in consumer sentiment across multiple platforms, allowing businesses to tailor their marketing messages and campaigns to resonate with their target audience. Additionally,

AI can help in predicting consumer behavior, enabling marketers to anticipate needs and adapt their strategies accordingly.

Furthermore, the insights gained from social listening and sentiment analysis can inform product development and innovation. By understanding customer feedback and preferences, businesses can create products that better align with market demands. This data-driven approach not only enhances the customer experience but also fosters brand loyalty. Companies that actively listen to their customers and respond to their sentiments are more likely to build a positive brand image and cultivate long-term relationships with their audience.

In conclusion, social listening and sentiment analysis represent a significant evolution in marketing strategies, particularly in an age dominated by digital communication. For business professionals, harnessing these tools is crucial for gaining a competitive advantage. As the marketing landscape continues to evolve, the ability to understand and respond to consumer sentiment will be essential for driving engagement, improving customer loyalty, and ultimately achieving business success. By embracing these technologies, companies can transform raw data into actionable insights, leading to more informed decision-making and strategic marketing initiatives.

Targeted Advertising with AI

Targeted advertising has evolved significantly with the integration of artificial intelligence (AI) technologies. Businesses are now able to analyze vast amounts of data to identify specific consumer segments and tailor their marketing strategies accordingly. This precision enables companies to deliver personalized messages to consumers at the right time and through the right channels. AI algorithms can sift through demographic information, online behavior, and purchase history to create highly targeted advertising campaigns that resonate with individual preferences and needs.

One of the key advantages of using AI in targeted advertising is the ability to predict consumer behavior. Machine learning algorithms can analyze patterns in data that human marketers might overlook, allowing businesses to anticipate what products or services a consumer is likely to be interested in. Predictive analytics can segment audiences more effectively, ensuring that marketing efforts are focused on those most likely to convert. As a result, companies can achieve higher return on investment (ROI) from their advertising spend by reaching consumers with relevant offers that meet their immediate needs.

Moreover, AI-driven targeted advertising enhances real-time optimization of ad campaigns. With AI, businesses can monitor campaign performance and make adjustments on the fly. This means that if a particular ad isn't performing as expected, marketers can quickly change their approach based on data insights. This agility allows companies to stay ahead of market trends and consumer preferences, ensuring that their advertising remains relevant and engaging. The continuous learning aspect of AI systems means that each iteration of a campaign can be more effective than the last.

However, the implementation of AI in targeted advertising is not without its challenges. Privacy concerns surrounding data collection and usage are paramount. Businesses must navigate regulations such as GDPR and CCPA while ensuring that they maintain consumer trust. Transparency in how data is collected and utilized for advertising purposes is essential. Companies that prioritize ethical considerations in their AI strategies are likely to build stronger relationships with their customers, ultimately leading to better brand loyalty and engagement.

In conclusion, targeted advertising powered by AI presents a transformative opportunity for businesses to enhance their marketing efforts. By leveraging data analytics, predictive modeling, and real-time optimization, companies can create personalized advertising experiences that drive consumer engagement and increase sales. As the landscape of digital marketing continues to evolve, the integration of AI will remain a critical component for businesses aiming to maintain a competitive edge in the marketplace. Embracing these technologies thoughtfully will enable organizations to not only meet but exceed consumer expectations in an increasingly personalized world.

Influencer Marketing in the AI Era

Influencer marketing has evolved dramatically with the advent of artificial intelligence, transforming how brands connect with consumers. In the AI era, businesses can leverage sophisticated algorithms to identify the most relevant influencers for their target audiences. This data-driven approach allows for a more strategic selection process, ensuring that brands partner with influencers whose followers align closely with their market demographics. By utilizing AI tools for sentiment analysis and audience insights, companies can refine their marketing strategies to resonate more effectively with potential customers.

AI also enhances content creation and curation, enabling influencers to produce engaging material that appeals to their followers while aligning with brand messaging. Advanced AI technologies can analyze trends in real-time, allowing influencers to stay ahead of the curve and create content that reflects the latest consumer interests. This leads to more authentic and timely interactions between brands and their audiences. By automating routine tasks, influencers can focus on creativity and engagement, enhancing the overall effectiveness of their marketing efforts.

Moreover, AI facilitates performance measurement and analysis in influencer campaigns. Businesses can track engagement metrics, conversion rates, and overall campaign ROI with greater precision. Machine learning algorithms can predict which types of content will perform best and provide recommendations for future campaigns. This level of insight allows brands to make data-backed decisions, optimizing their influencer partnerships for maximum impact and continuously improving their marketing strategies.

The integration of AI in influencer marketing also raises new challenges. Issues such as authenticity, transparency, and ethical considerations come to the forefront as brands navigate relationships with influencers. Consumers are increasingly aware of sponsored content and expect transparency regarding partnerships. Brands must ensure that their influencer collaborations are genuine and resonate with their audience's values to maintain trust and credibility. AI can assist in monitoring influencer activities to ensure compliance with advertising regulations and ethical standards.

As businesses continue to adapt to the changing landscape of marketing, the role of influencers in the AI era will remain pivotal. The combination of human creativity and AI-driven insights creates a powerful synergy that can drive brand awareness and consumer engagement. By embracing these advancements, companies can not only enhance their influencer marketing strategies but also position themselves competitively in the ever-evolving digital marketplace. The future of marketing lies in the ability to harness the potential of AI while maintaining authentic connections with consumers through trusted influencers.

Chapter 5: Customer Experience and AI

Chatbots and Virtual Assistants

Chatbots and virtual assistants have emerged as transformative tools in the landscape of marketing and advertising, enabling businesses to engage with customers in real-time and streamline various processes. These AI-driven technologies offer not only improved customer service but also enhanced data collection, allowing businesses to understand consumer preferences and behaviors more deeply. As companies strive to differentiate themselves in a competitive market, integrating chatbots and virtual assistants into their strategies has become essential for fostering meaningful interactions with audiences.

The capabilities of chatbots extend beyond simple customer inquiries. Advanced chatbots utilize natural language processing and machine learning algorithms to provide personalized recommendations and support. This personalization can significantly enhance the customer experience, making interactions feel more human-like and relevant. For instance, when a customer interacts with a chatbot on a retail website, the bot can analyze previous purchases and browsing history to suggest products that align with the individual's preferences, thereby driving sales and increasing customer satisfaction.

Virtual assistants, on the other hand, are often integrated into broader marketing strategies and can manage tasks such as scheduling, reminders, and even social media management. These tools help businesses maintain a consistent online presence while freeing up human resources for more strategic initiatives. By automating routine tasks, virtual assistants allow marketing teams to focus on content creation, campaign analysis, and strategic planning, ultimately leading to more effective marketing efforts and improved return on investment.

Moreover, chatbots and virtual assistants can play a pivotal role in gathering and analyzing customer data. By tracking interactions and user feedback, businesses can gain valuable insights into consumer behavior and preferences. This data-driven approach enables companies to refine their marketing strategies, ensuring they resonate with target audiences. Additionally, the ability to analyze real-time data allows for quick adjustments to campaigns, maximizing their effectiveness and relevance in an ever-changing market.

As businesses continue to navigate the digital landscape, the integration of chatbots and virtual assistants will be a key driver of innovation and customer engagement. With their ability to provide immediate responses, personalized experiences, and valuable data insights, these technologies are not merely enhancements but essential components of a modern marketing strategy. By leveraging AI in this way, businesses can gain a competitive advantage, positioning themselves as forward-thinking entities in an increasingly crowded marketplace.

Enhanced Customer Support

The integration of artificial intelligence in customer support is transforming how businesses interact with their clients. AI technologies, such as chatbots and virtual assistants, enable companies to provide immediate responses to customer inquiries, significantly reducing wait times and increasing satisfaction. These tools can handle a multitude of interactions simultaneously, allowing businesses to scale their support efforts without sacrificing quality. Through natural language processing and machine learning, AI can understand and respond to customer queries with human-like accuracy, ensuring that the support experience is both efficient and effective.

AI-powered customer support systems also offer valuable insights into customer behavior and preferences. By analyzing interactions, businesses can identify common pain points and frequently asked questions, which can inform product development and marketing strategies. This data-driven approach allows companies to tailor their offerings to meet customer needs better. In addition, AI can track customer sentiment in real-time, enabling businesses to respond proactively to issues before they escalate, thus enhancing customer loyalty and trust.

Another significant advantage of AI in customer support is its ability to provide 24/7 availability. Customers today expect support at any hour, and AI ensures that assistance is always accessible, regardless of time zones or business hours. This constant availability not only improves customer satisfaction but also allows businesses to capture leads and resolve issues outside traditional working hours, maximizing operational efficiency. The ability to engage customers at their convenience can lead to increased sales and a stronger competitive edge in the market.

Moreover, AI can facilitate personalized customer experiences. By leveraging data from previous interactions, AI systems can provide tailored recommendations and solutions, creating a more engaging and relevant support experience. This level of personalization fosters a deeper connection between the customer and the brand, as clients feel understood and valued. As a result, businesses can enhance customer retention and encourage repeat purchases, which are crucial components of long-term success in a competitive marketplace.

Lastly, the implementation of AI in customer support can lead to significant cost savings for businesses. By automating routine inquiries and freeing up human agents to handle more complex issues, companies can optimize their workforce and reduce operational costs. This efficiency not only allows for a more streamlined support process but also enables businesses to allocate resources to other critical areas such as marketing and product innovation. As organizations continue to embrace AI technology, the potential for enhanced customer support will play a vital role in driving growth and maintaining a competitive advantage in the rapidly evolving business landscape.

Tailoring the Customer Journey

Tailoring the customer journey is a crucial aspect of modern marketing strategies, particularly in an era dominated by artificial intelligence. Businesses now have access to vast amounts of data, which enables them to understand customer behaviors, preferences, and pain points more comprehensively than ever before. An effective customer journey is not a one-size-fits-all approach; it requires personalization at every touchpoint. By leveraging AI, organizations can analyze customer interactions across various channels and create tailored experiences that resonate with individual users.

One of the primary ways to tailor the customer journey is through predictive analytics. AI algorithms can process historical data to forecast future customer behaviors, allowing businesses to anticipate needs and personalize offerings. For instance, an e-commerce platform can utilize predictive models to suggest products based on past purchases and browsing history. This not only enhances the customer experience by providing relevant recommendations but also increases conversion rates and customer loyalty. By understanding what customers are likely to need or want next, businesses can create a seamless shopping experience that feels intuitive and personalized.

Another critical element in tailoring the customer journey is real-time personalization. AI technologies can analyze customer data in real time, enabling businesses to adjust their messaging and offers instantaneously based on current behaviors. For example, if a customer is browsing a website and hesitates at a particular product, AI systems can trigger personalized messages or offers to encourage the customer to proceed with the purchase. This level of responsiveness can significantly improve engagement rates and drive sales. By ensuring that interactions are relevant and timely, businesses can create a more compelling customer journey that keeps users engaged.

Furthermore, AI can enhance the customer journey through automation. Chatbots and virtual assistants can provide immediate support and guidance, addressing customer inquiries and concerns without human intervention. This not only improves efficiency but also ensures that customers receive consistent and accurate information. By streamlining communication and making assistance readily available, businesses can reduce friction in the customer journey, allowing users to navigate their experiences with ease. Automation powered by AI can play a vital role in maintaining customer satisfaction and fostering long-term relationships.

Finally, monitoring and refining the customer journey is essential for ongoing success. AI tools can continuously track customer interactions, gathering insights that inform future strategies. By analyzing feedback and engagement metrics, businesses can identify areas for improvement and adapt their approaches accordingly. This iterative process ensures that the customer journey evolves alongside changing consumer preferences and market dynamics. Ultimately, tailoring the customer journey with the help of AI not only meets the needs of today's consumers but also positions businesses for sustained competitive advantage in a rapidly changing landscape.

Chapter 6: AI-Driven Marketing Automation

Streamlining Campaign Management

Streamlining campaign management is essential in the fast-paced realm of marketing and advertising, particularly with the integration of artificial intelligence. Business professionals must recognize that traditional campaign management methods can be cumbersome and time-consuming, often leading to inefficiencies that detract from overall marketing effectiveness. By leveraging AI-driven tools and solutions, organizations can transform their campaign management processes, leading to enhanced productivity, improved targeting, and ultimately, better returns on investment.

AI technologies can automate various aspects of campaign management, from planning and execution to monitoring and analysis. For instance, predictive analytics can help marketers identify the most promising audience segments based on historical data and trends. This capability allows for more precise targeting, ensuring that campaigns reach the right consumers at the right time. Additionally, AI algorithms can optimize ad placements in real-time, adjusting bids and targeting criteria based on the performance of different channels and demographics. This level of automation not only saves time but also maximizes the effectiveness of marketing spend.

Another significant advantage of AI in campaign management is the ability to gather and analyze vast amounts of data quickly. With machine learning models, businesses can process consumer behavior data, social media interactions, and engagement metrics to derive actionable insights. These insights can inform strategic decisions, such as which messaging resonates most with different audience segments, allowing marketers to tailor their campaigns for greater impact. Furthermore, AI can continuously learn from ongoing campaigns, refining strategies based on real-time performance, which is a marked improvement over static, one-size-fits-all approaches.

Collaboration among marketing teams can also be enhanced through AI-powered tools. By providing a centralized platform for campaign management, team members can access shared insights, project updates, and performance metrics in real-time. This transparency fosters a more cohesive approach to campaign development and execution, breaking down silos that can hinder collaboration. Additionally, AI can facilitate communication between teams by offering chatbots and virtual assistants that streamline information sharing and task management, allowing professionals to focus more on creative and strategic aspects of their work.

Finally, the integration of AI into campaign management not only boosts efficiency but also enhances the agility of marketing operations. In an ever-changing market landscape, the ability to pivot quickly in response to new trends or consumer feedback is crucial. AI-driven tools can help marketers evaluate the performance of campaigns on an ongoing basis, enabling rapid adjustments that keep strategies aligned with current market conditions. This adaptability is vital for maintaining a competitive advantage, as businesses that can respond swiftly to changes are better positioned to capture emerging opportunities and mitigate risks.

Email Marketing Optimization

Email marketing optimization is a critical component of any effective marketing strategy, particularly for business professionals looking to leverage artificial intelligence to enhance engagement and conversion rates. The first step in optimizing email marketing efforts involves understanding the target audience. By employing AI-driven analytics tools, businesses can gather insights into recipient behaviors, preferences, and demographics. This data enables marketers to segment their email lists effectively, ensuring that the right messages reach the right people at the right time. As a result, tailored content can be created that speaks directly to the needs and interests of each segment, leading to improved open and click-through rates.

Another essential aspect of email marketing optimization is A/B testing. This method allows marketers to experiment with different subject lines, content formats, images, and calls to action to determine what resonates best with their audience. AI can significantly enhance this process by rapidly analyzing the performance of various email elements and providing actionable insights. By systematically testing and refining email components, businesses can incrementally improve their campaigns and achieve higher engagement levels. This data-driven approach ensures that decisions are based on real-time feedback, maximizing the effectiveness of email marketing strategies.

Personalization is a key trend in email marketing that can dramatically enhance user experience. Utilizing AI technologies, businesses can create highly personalized email campaigns that reflect individual recipient behaviors and preferences. For instance, AI algorithms can analyze past purchase history, browsing behavior, and engagement patterns to recommend products or content specifically suited to each recipient. This level of personalization not only fosters a stronger connection between the brand and the consumer but also increases the likelihood of conversion. As AI continues to evolve, the ability to deliver tailored content in real-time will become increasingly sophisticated, allowing for even deeper customer relationships.

Automation plays a pivotal role in optimizing email marketing campaigns, making it easier to manage large-scale marketing efforts without sacrificing quality. By implementing AI-driven automation tools, businesses can schedule emails, trigger campaigns based on user interactions, and follow up with leads at appropriate intervals. This not only saves time but also ensures that communication is consistent and relevant. For example, automated workflows can send welcome emails to new subscribers or follow-up messages to customers who have abandoned their shopping carts. Such timely interventions can significantly enhance customer engagement and retention.

Finally, measuring and analyzing the success of email marketing campaigns is crucial for ongoing optimization. AI can assist in tracking key performance metrics such as open rates, click-through rates, conversion rates, and unsubscribe rates. By leveraging advanced analytics, businesses can gain insights into what strategies are working and what areas require improvement. This continuous feedback loop allows marketers to adapt their email campaigns dynamically, ensuring they remain relevant and effective in a rapidly changing digital landscape. Ultimately, a commitment to email marketing optimization, powered by AI, enables businesses to stay competitive and drive better results in their marketing endeavors.

Performance Tracking and Reporting

Performance tracking and reporting are essential components of any successful marketing strategy, particularly in the context of leveraging artificial intelligence. As businesses increasingly rely on digital marketing channels, the need for precise metrics to evaluate campaign effectiveness has never been more critical. AI technologies offer sophisticated tools that can automate data collection, analyze performance in real-time, and generate insightful reports. This allows marketing professionals to make informed decisions based on accurate data rather than intuition alone.

One of the primary advantages of AI in performance tracking is its ability to consolidate vast amounts of data from various sources. Traditional methods often involve manual entry and analysis, which can be time-consuming and prone to errors. However, AI-driven platforms can seamlessly integrate data from social media, email campaigns, website analytics, and customer relationship management systems. This holistic view of marketing performance enables organizations to identify trends and anomalies quickly, facilitating timely adjustments to optimize ongoing campaigns.

Additionally, AI enhances the granularity of performance insights. With advanced algorithms, businesses can segment their audience more effectively, allowing for tailored reporting that highlights the performance of specific demographics or customer behaviors. This level of detail is invaluable when assessing the efficacy of different marketing strategies. For instance, an AI system may reveal that a particular audience segment responds more positively to video content than static image ads, prompting marketers to reallocate resources accordingly.

Reporting tools powered by AI also contribute to greater accountability within marketing teams. Automated reports can be generated at regular intervals, providing stakeholders with consistent updates on campaign performance. This transparency not only fosters a culture of data-driven decision-making but also allows for quick identification of underperforming initiatives. By establishing clear performance benchmarks and using AI to track progress against these goals, businesses can ensure that marketing efforts align with overall organizational objectives.

Finally, the integration of AI in performance tracking and reporting allows for predictive analytics, which can significantly enhance future marketing strategies. By analyzing historical data, AI can identify patterns and forecast potential outcomes of future campaigns. This predictive capability empowers businesses to allocate budgets more effectively, develop targeted messaging, and anticipate market shifts. As a result, organizations that embrace AI for performance tracking are better positioned to respond proactively to changes in consumer behavior and market conditions, ultimately gaining a competitive advantage in the evolving landscape of marketing and advertising.

Chapter 7: Ethical Considerations in AI Marketing

Data Privacy and Security

Data privacy and security are crucial considerations for businesses leveraging artificial intelligence in marketing and advertising. The integration of AI technologies into marketing strategies enables companies to gather and analyze vast amounts of consumer data, allowing for personalized marketing campaigns that can significantly enhance customer engagement. However, this data-driven approach raises significant concerns regarding the collection, storage, and utilization of sensitive consumer information. Business professionals must prioritize data privacy and security to maintain consumer trust and comply with evolving regulations.

The regulatory landscape surrounding data privacy is continuously changing, with laws such as the General Data Protection Regulation (GDPR) in Europe and the California Consumer Privacy Act (CCPA) in the United States setting strict guidelines for data handling. These regulations require businesses to obtain explicit consent from consumers before collecting their data, providing transparency about how their information will be used, and allowing them to access or delete their data upon request. Failure to comply with these regulations can result in severe financial penalties and damage to a company's reputation, underscoring the importance of incorporating robust data privacy measures into marketing strategies.

In addition to regulatory compliance, organizations must implement technical safeguards to protect consumer data from breaches and unauthorized access. This includes utilizing encryption, secure data storage solutions, and regular security audits to identify vulnerabilities within their systems. Investing in cybersecurity measures is essential, as data breaches not only jeopardize sensitive consumer information but also erode consumer confidence in the brand. A proactive approach to data security can serve as a competitive advantage, reassuring customers that their information is handled with the utmost care and integrity.

Moreover, adopting ethical guidelines for AI-driven marketing practices can further enhance data privacy and security. This includes establishing clear policies for data usage, ensuring that AI algorithms do not inadvertently perpetuate biases or discriminate against certain consumer groups. By prioritizing ethical considerations, businesses can foster a culture of accountability and transparency, ultimately leading to stronger relationships with their customers. Ethical AI practices can also differentiate a brand in a crowded marketplace, attracting consumers who value responsible business practices.

Finally, continuous education and training for employees are vital in maintaining a culture of data privacy and security. Business professionals must stay informed about the latest developments in data protection laws and best practices for safeguarding consumer information. Regular training sessions can equip employees with the knowledge and skills necessary to recognize potential security threats and respond appropriately. By embedding a strong commitment to data privacy and security within the organization's culture, businesses can not only comply with regulations but also build lasting trust with their customers, ultimately enhancing their competitive advantage in the market.

Transparency in AI Algorithms

Transparency in AI algorithms is becoming increasingly critical in the marketing and advertising sectors. As businesses adopt AI technologies to streamline their operations and enhance customer engagement, understanding the decision-making processes of these algorithms is essential. Transparency involves providing insights into how AI systems make decisions, the data they utilize, and the underlying models that drive their predictions. This openness fosters trust among consumers and stakeholders, ensuring that marketing practices remain ethical and accountable.

One of the primary benefits of transparency in AI algorithms is the ability to build consumer trust. In an era where data privacy concerns are paramount, businesses that clearly communicate how they use AI can alleviate fears related to data misuse. When consumers are informed about how their data is collected, processed, and employed in marketing strategies, they are more likely to engage with brands. For instance, when a customer receives personalized recommendations, understanding that these suggestions come from a transparent algorithm can enhance their overall experience and foster loyalty.

Moreover, transparency allows businesses to maintain compliance with regulatory frameworks governing data use and consumer protection. Many regions are implementing strict laws around data privacy, such as the General Data Protection Regulation (GDPR) in Europe. By ensuring that AI algorithms are transparent, companies can demonstrate their commitment to ethical practices and compliance with these regulations. This not only helps avoid potential legal repercussions but also positions the organization as a responsible leader in the marketplace, differentiating it from competitors that may not prioritize ethical AI practices.

In addition to fostering trust and compliance, transparency in AI algorithms can drive better decision-making within organizations. When marketing teams understand how AI systems function and the rationale behind their outputs, they can make more informed choices regarding campaign strategies and resource allocation. This understanding enables marketers to interpret AI-generated insights accurately, leading to more effective targeting and engagement efforts. As a result, organizations can optimize their marketing campaigns to achieve higher returns on investment and ultimately enhance their competitive advantage.

Lastly, the demand for transparency in AI is reshaping the relationship between consumers and brands. As consumers become more aware of AI's role in their interactions with businesses, they are increasingly seeking brands that prioritize ethical practices. By adopting transparent AI algorithms, companies can engage in meaningful conversations with their audience, addressing concerns and demonstrating their commitment to responsible marketing. This shift not only benefits consumers but also reinforces a brand's reputation and fosters long-term relationships, creating a win-win scenario in the evolving landscape of marketing and advertising.

Building Trust with Consumers

Building trust with consumers is essential for any marketing strategy, especially in an era where artificial intelligence plays a significant role in shaping consumer interactions. Trust is the foundation of customer loyalty and long-term engagement, as it fosters a sense of reliability between a brand and its audience. In the context of AI in marketing, businesses must navigate the complexities of data privacy, transparency, and ethical considerations to cultivate an environment of trust. Understanding these components is vital for professionals looking to leverage AI effectively.

One of the primary ways to build trust with consumers is through transparency. Businesses should be open about how they collect, use, and store consumer data. Providing clear information about data practices not only complies with regulations like GDPR but also reassures consumers that their personal information is being handled responsibly. AI tools can facilitate this transparency by simplifying the communication of privacy policies and data usage, thus making it easier for consumers to understand their rights and the measures in place to protect their information.

Additionally, personalization powered by AI can enhance trust when executed thoughtfully. Consumers increasingly expect tailored experiences, and AI can analyze vast amounts of data to deliver personalized content and recommendations. However, it is crucial to strike a balance between personalization and privacy. Overstepping boundaries can lead to feelings of intrusion rather than engagement. By employing AI responsibly and allowing consumers to control their preferences, businesses can enhance their relationship with customers while reinforcing trust.

Consumer feedback mechanisms also play a critical role in building trust. AI technologies can analyze customer sentiments and behaviors in real-time, allowing businesses to respond proactively to concerns and adapt their strategies accordingly. Engaging with consumers through surveys, social media, and direct communication not only shows that a company values their opinions but also demonstrates a commitment to continuous improvement. This responsiveness builds credibility and reinforces the brand's reliability in the eyes of consumers.

Lastly, ethical marketing practices should be at the forefront of any AI-driven strategy. Businesses must ensure that their AI systems are designed to avoid biases and promote fairness. By establishing ethical guidelines and regularly auditing AI processes, companies can enhance their integrity and build stronger relationships with consumers. In a marketplace increasingly influenced by technology, a company's commitment to ethical practices can be a significant differentiator, further enhancing consumer trust and loyalty.

Chapter 8: Case Studies of Successful AI Implementation

Leading Brands Utilizing AI

Leading brands are increasingly utilizing artificial intelligence to enhance their marketing strategies and gain a competitive edge. Companies such as Amazon, Netflix, and Coca-Cola have integrated AI into their operations to streamline processes, personalize customer experiences, and improve decision-making. These brands exemplify how AI can transform traditional marketing methods into data-driven, customer-centric approaches. By harnessing vast amounts of data, these companies are able to understand consumer behaviors and preferences, allowing them to tailor their marketing efforts more effectively.

Amazon, for instance, employs AI algorithms to analyze customer data and recommend products based on individual shopping habits. This personalization not only enhances the customer experience but also drives sales, as customers are more likely to purchase items that align with their interests. Additionally, Amazon uses AI for dynamic pricing strategies, adjusting prices in real-time based on demand, competitor pricing, and other factors. This ability to respond swiftly to market changes helps Amazon maintain its position as a leader in e-commerce.

Netflix has revolutionized content consumption through the use of AI algorithms that analyze user viewing patterns. By understanding what content resonates with different demographics, Netflix can suggest shows and movies that align with viewer preferences, ultimately increasing user engagement and retention. Furthermore, Netflix employs AI in content creation, utilizing predictive analytics to identify trends and inform decisions about which shows to produce. This strategic use of AI not only optimizes their content library but also minimizes the risk of investing in unsuccessful productions.

Coca-Cola has also embraced AI in its marketing efforts, using machine learning to analyze consumer data and optimize advertising campaigns. The brand leverages AI to understand the effectiveness of its marketing channels and to predict consumer responses to various advertisements. By implementing AI-driven insights, Coca-Cola can create more targeted and relevant advertising strategies, ensuring that their messages resonate with their audience. This data-driven approach enables the brand to allocate marketing resources more efficiently and enhance overall campaign performance.

The integration of AI in marketing is not limited to these leading brands; it is a trend that is expanding across various industries. Companies are recognizing the importance of data analytics and automated systems in understanding consumer behavior and optimizing marketing strategies. As AI technology continues to evolve, businesses that adopt these innovations will likely gain a significant advantage over competitors that remain reliant on traditional marketing methods. By investing in AI, brands can enhance their marketing capabilities, improve customer relationships, and drive long-term growth in an increasingly competitive marketplace.

Lessons Learned from Failures

Failures in marketing can often serve as the most valuable teachers, providing insights that are crucial for future success. In the fast-evolving landscape of AI in marketing and advertising, understanding the lessons learned from missteps can help business professionals refine their strategies and avoid repeating the same mistakes. One key takeaway is the importance of data-driven decision-making. Many organizations have stumbled by relying on assumptions rather than analyzing consumer data. By leveraging AI to gather and interpret data, businesses can gain a clearer picture of consumer preferences and behaviors, allowing them to make informed choices that resonate with their target audience.

Another lesson from failures is the necessity of adaptability. Companies that have rigidly adhered to their initial marketing strategies often found themselves outpaced by competitors who embraced flexibility and innovation. The rapid advancements in AI technology require marketers to remain agile, continuously testing and iterating their campaigns based on real-time feedback. Those who have failed to pivot have experienced diminished relevance in the marketplace. Embracing a culture of experimentation and being willing to adjust tactics in response to performance metrics can significantly enhance the effectiveness of marketing efforts.

Moreover, the significance of understanding the customer journey cannot be overstated. Many marketing failures stem from a lack of insight into how consumers interact with brands across various touchpoints. AI tools can provide a comprehensive view of the customer journey, highlighting key moments that influence purchasing decisions. By analyzing these interactions, businesses can tailor their marketing messages to meet consumer needs more effectively. This understanding fosters stronger connections between brands and consumers, ultimately leading to higher conversion rates and customer loyalty.

Collaboration across departments is another critical lesson learned from past failures. When marketing teams operate in silos, opportunities for synergistic strategies can be lost. Successful campaigns often involve input from multiple departments, including sales, customer service, and product development. AI can facilitate this collaboration by providing a shared platform for data analysis and insights. By fostering a culture of teamwork and open communication, businesses can create integrated marketing strategies that leverage the strengths of various teams, enhancing overall performance.

Finally, the importance of ethical considerations in AI marketing cannot be ignored. Several high-profile failures have arisen from practices that were perceived as invasive or manipulative. Businesses must prioritize transparency and ethical data use to build trust with consumers. By implementing ethical guidelines and ensuring that AI tools are used responsibly, companies can not only avoid backlash but also enhance their brand reputation. Learning from past mistakes in this regard can lead to more sustainable marketing practices that resonate positively with consumers, ultimately driving long-term success.

Future Trends in AI Marketing

The landscape of AI marketing is continuously evolving, and several key trends are poised to shape its future. One of the most significant trends is the increased integration of artificial intelligence with customer relationship management (CRM) systems. Businesses are leveraging AI to analyze customer data more effectively, enabling them to create highly personalized marketing strategies. These advancements allow companies to predict customer behavior and preferences with greater accuracy, leading to tailored marketing campaigns that resonate more deeply with target audiences. As AI technology becomes more sophisticated, we can expect CRM systems to become increasingly intuitive, facilitating seamless interactions between brands and consumers.

Another trend gaining traction is the rise of AI-driven content creation. As businesses strive to produce high-quality content at scale, AI tools are stepping in to assist with everything from blog posts to social media updates. These tools can analyze audience engagement data to determine what types of content are most effective, ultimately helping marketers craft messages that capture attention and drive conversions. Moreover, advancements in natural language processing (NLP) will enable AI to generate content that feels more human-like, reducing the gap between automated and human-generated material. This evolution will empower marketers to focus on strategy and creativity while relying on AI for efficiency.

The use of predictive analytics in marketing is also expected to grow significantly. By harnessing vast amounts of data, AI can identify patterns and trends that inform future marketing strategies. This capability allows businesses to anticipate customer needs and adjust their offerings accordingly. For instance, AI can help identify which products are likely to become popular based on historical data, seasonal trends, or emerging consumer behaviors. As predictive analytics become more sophisticated, companies will be better equipped to make data-driven decisions that enhance their marketing efforts and improve overall customer satisfaction.

Moreover, the ethical implications of AI in marketing will come under increased scrutiny. As companies adopt AI technologies, they must navigate concerns related to data privacy and consumer trust. Transparency in how AI algorithms operate and how data is used will be crucial for maintaining customer loyalty. Companies will need to establish clear guidelines and ethical standards for their AI marketing practices, ensuring that they respect customer privacy while still delivering personalized experiences. This focus on ethical AI will not only help build consumer trust but also differentiate brands in a crowded marketplace.

Lastly, the integration of AI with emerging technologies such as augmented reality (AR) and virtual reality (VR) presents exciting opportunities for marketers. These technologies can create immersive experiences that engage consumers in novel ways. For instance, brands can utilize AI-powered AR applications to allow customers to visualize products in their own environment before making a purchase. This innovative approach enhances the shopping experience and can significantly reduce return rates. As businesses continue to explore the potential of AR and VR in conjunction with AI, we can anticipate a new era of marketing that prioritizes engagement, interactivity, and customer satisfaction.

Chapter 9: Building an AI-Ready Marketing Team

Skills and Knowledge Required

The landscape of marketing and advertising is rapidly evolving, heavily influenced by advancements in artificial intelligence. To effectively leverage AI for competitive advantage, business professionals must possess a unique set of skills and knowledge that enables them to navigate this transformative environment. Understanding the fundamental principles of AI and its application in marketing is crucial. This includes familiarity with machine learning algorithms, data analytics, and natural language processing, as these technologies are pivotal in driving personalized marketing strategies and optimizing customer engagement.

In addition to technical skills, professionals must develop a strong foundation in data management and analytics. The ability to collect, analyze, and interpret large datasets is essential for making informed marketing decisions. Business professionals should be adept at using various analytical tools and platforms that facilitate data-driven insights. This knowledge enables marketers to segment audiences, predict consumer behavior, and measure campaign effectiveness. Furthermore, understanding data privacy regulations and ethical considerations surrounding data usage is increasingly important, as consumers are more aware of their digital footprint and demand greater transparency.

Creativity and strategic thinking remain critical components in the AI-enhanced marketing landscape. While AI can automate many processes, the human touch is irreplaceable when it comes to crafting compelling narratives and engaging content. Professionals must blend creative skills with analytical insights to design marketing campaigns that resonate with target audiences. This involves not only understanding consumer preferences but also predicting trends and adapting strategies accordingly. The ability to think strategically about how AI tools can enhance creative processes will set successful marketers apart in a crowded marketplace.

Collaboration and communication skills are also paramount in this new era of marketing. As AI technologies become integrated into various marketing functions, professionals must work effectively with cross-functional teams, including data scientists, IT specialists, and creative designers. Being able to articulate the vision and benefits of AI-driven initiatives to stakeholders is vital for securing buy-in and fostering a culture of innovation within organizations. Strong interpersonal skills will facilitate collaboration, ensuring that diverse perspectives are considered in the development and execution of marketing strategies.

Lastly, continuous learning and adaptability are essential traits for business professionals in the realm of AI marketing. The rapid pace of technological change means that staying current with emerging trends, tools, and methodologies is not optional but a necessity. Engaging in professional development opportunities, attending industry conferences, and participating in relevant online courses can help professionals enhance their expertise. Embracing a mindset of lifelong learning allows marketers to remain competitive and innovative, ultimately positioning themselves and their organizations for sustained success in an AI-driven marketplace.

Fostering a Culture of Innovation

Fostering a culture of innovation is essential for businesses looking to stay competitive in the rapidly evolving landscape of AI marketing and advertising. Organizations must create an environment where creativity is encouraged, and risk-taking is supported. This involves not only empowering employees to share their ideas but also providing them with the resources and time to explore these concepts. Encouraging collaboration across different departments can lead to fresh insights and innovative solutions that harness the potential of artificial intelligence.

Leadership plays a crucial role in establishing a culture of innovation. Business professionals must model the behaviors they wish to see within their teams, demonstrating openness to new ideas and a willingness to experiment. This can be achieved by recognizing and rewarding innovative thinking and by providing opportunities for team members to engage in creative problem-solving sessions. By cultivating an atmosphere where employees feel valued for their contributions, organizations can enhance their ability to leverage AI in marketing strategies effectively.

Training and development initiatives can further reinforce a culture of innovation. As AI technologies continue to evolve, businesses must ensure that their teams are equipped with the necessary skills to adapt to these changes. This can involve ongoing education on emerging AI tools and techniques, as well as fostering a mindset that embraces continuous learning. Workshops, seminars, and collaborative projects can all serve as platforms for knowledge sharing, enabling employees to stay ahead of industry trends and implement innovative marketing solutions.

Additionally, embracing a customer-centric approach can drive innovation within marketing and advertising efforts. By actively seeking feedback from customers and using data analytics to understand their preferences, businesses can tailor their AI strategies to meet evolving demands. Encouraging a culture where employees prioritize the customer experience can lead to the development of groundbreaking campaigns and products that resonate with target audiences. This alignment of innovation with customer needs is critical for maintaining relevance in the market.

Finally, organizations must be prepared to iterate on their ideas and embrace failure as part of the innovation process. Not every initiative will yield successful results, but each experience offers valuable lessons that can inform future strategies. By adopting an agile mindset, businesses can quickly pivot and refine their approaches based on real-time feedback and performance metrics. A culture that embraces experimentation and views setbacks as opportunities for growth will ultimately foster a sustainable environment for innovation, allowing companies to capitalize on the transformative potential of AI in their marketing and advertising efforts.

Collaborating with AI Experts

Collaborating with AI experts is a crucial strategy for businesses aiming to leverage artificial intelligence in their marketing and advertising efforts. As AI technology continues to evolve, the complexity of its applications increases, making it essential for organizations to partner with professionals who have a deep understanding of AI methodologies and tools. These experts can provide insights into the latest trends and innovations, helping businesses stay ahead of the competition by integrating AI solutions that are tailored to their specific needs.

AI experts can assist in identifying the most suitable technologies for a company's marketing objectives. With a multitude of platforms available, ranging from machine learning algorithms for data analysis to natural language processing for customer interaction, selecting the right tools can be overwhelming. Collaborating with AI specialists allows businesses to navigate this landscape effectively. They can evaluate the current state of a company's marketing strategies and recommend AI applications that will enhance efficiency, improve customer engagement, and ultimately drive sales.

Furthermore, AI experts play a pivotal role in implementing and managing AI systems within an organization. Their expertise ensures that the integration process is seamless, minimizing disruptions to existing workflows. They can provide training for staff members, ensuring that the team is well-equipped to use the new tools and technologies effectively. This training not only enhances the skill set of employees but also fosters a culture of innovation within the organization, encouraging team members to embrace AI as a valuable asset rather than a daunting challenge.

Data privacy and ethical considerations are increasingly important in the realm of AI in marketing. Collaborating with AI experts can help businesses navigate these complex issues. Experts can guide organizations in establishing frameworks that ensure compliance with regulations while maintaining customer trust. They can also help create ethical AI policies that prioritize transparency and responsible use of data, which are critical in maintaining a positive brand reputation. By addressing these concerns proactively, businesses can mitigate risks associated with AI adoption.

In conclusion, the collaboration between businesses and AI experts is not just beneficial; it is essential for success in today's competitive marketing landscape. By tapping into the knowledge and skills of these professionals, organizations can enhance their marketing strategies, implement cutting-edge technologies, and navigate the ethical landscape of AI. This partnership not only positions businesses to leverage AI for immediate gains but also prepares them for future advancements, ensuring long-term growth and sustainability in the rapidly evolving world of marketing and advertising.

Chapter 10: The Future of Marketing with AI

Emerging Technologies and Their Impact

Emerging technologies are transforming the landscape of marketing and advertising, offering businesses innovative tools and strategies to enhance their competitive edge. Among these technologies, artificial intelligence (AI) stands out as a pivotal force reshaping how companies engage with consumers. AI enables brands to analyze vast amounts of data, derive actionable insights, and deliver personalized experiences at an unprecedented scale. As businesses embrace these advancements, understanding their implications and applications becomes essential for staying ahead in a rapidly evolving marketplace.

One of the most significant impacts of AI in marketing is its ability to improve customer segmentation and targeting. Traditional methods often relied on demographic data, but AI-driven analytics can sift through behavioral data, preferences, and even social media interactions to create more nuanced customer profiles. This precision allows marketers to craft highly targeted campaigns that resonate with specific audience segments. As a result, companies can optimize their advertising spend, enhance engagement rates, and ultimately drive higher conversion rates, leading to a more efficient marketing strategy.

Furthermore, the integration of AI chatbots and virtual assistants is revolutionizing customer service and engagement. These tools leverage natural language processing to interact with customers in real-time, providing instant responses to inquiries, guiding them through purchase decisions, and enhancing overall customer experience. By automating routine tasks and offering personalized assistance, businesses can not only reduce operational costs but also foster stronger relationships with consumers. This shift towards AI-driven customer service underscores the importance of integrating technology into the marketing mix for sustained success.

Predictive analytics is another area where emerging technologies are making a significant impact. By utilizing machine learning algorithms, businesses can forecast trends, consumer behavior, and market shifts with greater accuracy. This foresight enables marketers to proactively adjust their strategies, allocate resources more effectively, and anticipate customer needs. As a result, companies can stay ahead of the competition, ensuring they are not only reactive but also proactive in their marketing efforts. The ability to predict outcomes based on data-driven insights is becoming a crucial component of successful marketing strategies in the digital age.

Lastly, the rise of augmented reality (AR) and virtual reality (VR) technologies is creating immersive advertising experiences that captivate consumers in new ways. Brands are increasingly using AR and VR to offer interactive experiences, allowing potential customers to visualize products in their environments or engage with immersive storytelling. This innovative approach not only enhances brand awareness but also fosters deeper emotional connections with consumers. As these technologies continue to evolve, businesses that harness their potential will likely gain a significant advantage in engaging and retaining customers in a crowded marketplace.

Adapting to Rapid Changes

In the fast-evolving landscape of marketing and advertising, adapting to rapid changes is paramount for business professionals seeking to maintain a competitive edge. The integration of artificial intelligence (AI) into marketing strategies has transformed how companies engage with their audiences. Organizations must embrace this technological shift, recognizing that AI offers innovative solutions that can enhance customer experiences, streamline operations, and optimize marketing efforts. By understanding the dynamics of AI, professionals can better navigate the complexities of modern marketing.

One of the significant aspects of adapting to rapid changes is the ability to harness data effectively. AI enables the collection and analysis of vast amounts of data, providing insights that were previously unattainable. Business professionals can leverage this data to identify trends, understand consumer behavior, and segment their target audiences with greater precision. By utilizing AI-driven analytics, companies can make informed decisions that enhance their marketing strategies, ensuring they remain relevant in an ever-changing environment.

Moreover, the rise of AI has led to the emergence of new marketing channels and tools. Social media platforms, chatbots, and personalized advertising are just a few examples of how AI is reshaping customer interactions. Business professionals must stay informed about these developments to effectively engage consumers through the channels they prefer. Adapting to these changes involves continuous learning and experimentation, as marketers test new technologies and approaches to determine what resonates best with their audience.

Another critical factor in adapting to rapid changes is fostering a culture of innovation within organizations. Business professionals should encourage collaboration and creativity among teams to explore new AI applications and marketing strategies. This culture not only allows for quick adaptation to current trends but also positions companies to anticipate future changes. By promoting an environment where experimentation is valued, organizations can develop innovative marketing initiatives that leverage AI capabilities to their fullest potential.

Finally, it is essential for business professionals to prioritize ethical considerations in their marketing strategies. As AI technologies continue to evolve, concerns regarding data privacy and transparency have become increasingly prominent. Adapting to changes in consumer expectations around privacy requires a balanced approach that respects user data while leveraging AI to deliver personalized experiences. By prioritizing ethical practices, companies can build trust with their customers, ensuring long-term success in a rapidly changing marketing landscape.

Strategic Planning for a Competitive Edge

Strategic planning is essential for businesses aiming to gain a competitive edge in the rapidly evolving landscape of marketing and advertising, especially with the integration of artificial intelligence (AI). A well-structured strategic plan allows organizations to set clear objectives, allocate resources efficiently, and anticipate market trends. In the context of AI, this planning involves understanding how to harness its capabilities to improve decision-making, enhance customer experiences, and optimize marketing efforts. By aligning AI initiatives with broader business goals, companies can position themselves to capitalize on emerging opportunities and mitigate potential risks.

One of the first steps in strategic planning for leveraging AI in marketing is conducting a comprehensive market analysis. This includes assessing competitors' use of AI technologies, identifying gaps in the market, and understanding customer preferences. Business professionals must gather data from various sources, including consumer behavior analytics, social media trends, and industry reports. This information helps in identifying key performance indicators (KPIs) that align with AI initiatives, ensuring that the strategies developed are data-driven and focused on measurable outcomes. By continuously monitoring these metrics, organizations can adapt their approaches in real-time, ensuring agility in their marketing efforts.

Another critical component of strategic planning is the integration of AI tools across marketing functions. It is vital to evaluate which AI technologies can be effectively incorporated into existing marketing frameworks. This may include employing machine learning algorithms for predictive analytics, utilizing chatbots for enhanced customer engagement, or implementing automated content creation tools. By leveraging these technologies, businesses can streamline their operations, enhance personalization, and improve overall customer satisfaction. Furthermore, training staff to work alongside AI tools is essential for maximizing their potential and ensuring a seamless integration into daily workflows.

Collaboration fosters innovation, making it crucial for businesses to build partnerships that enhance their AI capabilities. Engaging with technology providers, academic institutions, and industry experts can provide valuable insights and resources. These collaborations can lead to the development of unique solutions tailored to specific marketing challenges. Moreover, sharing knowledge and best practices within these partnerships can accelerate the learning curve associated with AI implementation. As a result, businesses can cultivate a culture of innovation that not only enhances their marketing strategies but also positions them as leaders in their respective markets.

Finally, continuous evaluation and refinement of the strategic plan are necessary to maintain a competitive edge in the dynamic field of AI in marketing. This involves regularly revisiting objectives, assessing the effectiveness of AI initiatives, and making adjustments based on market feedback and technological advancements. By fostering a mindset of adaptability, organizations can ensure that their marketing strategies remain relevant and effective. Embracing a proactive approach to strategic planning not only enhances operational efficiency but also empowers businesses to stay ahead of their competitors in an increasingly AI-driven marketplace.

www.ingramcontent.com/pod-product-compliance
Lightning Source LLC
Chambersburg PA
CBHW070947220526
45471CB00007B/2923